T5-BSG-365

The Christmas Treasury

The Christmas Treasury

THE TWELVE DAYS OF CHRISTMAS

❖

THE NUTCRACKER

❖

THE NIGHT BEFORE CHRISTMAS

RUNNING PRESS
PHILADELPHIA · LONDON

A Running Press Miniature Edition™

© 1998 by Running Press

All rights reserved under the Pan-American and
International Copyright Conventions

Printed in China

*This book may not be reproduced in whole or in part, in any form
or by any means, electronic or mechanical, including photocopying,
recording, or by any information storage and retrieval system
now known or hereafter invented, without written
permission from the publisher.
The proprietary trade dress, including the size and format,
of this Running Press Miniature Edition™ is the property of
Running Press. It may not be used or reproduced without the
express written permission of Running Press.*

Library of Congress Cataloging-in-Publication Number
98-66654

ISBN 0-7624-0423-X

This book may be ordered by mail from the publisher.
Please include $1.00 for postage and handling.

But try your bookstore first!

Running Press Book Publishers
125 South Twenty-second Street
Philadelphia, Pennsylvania 19103-4399

The Twelve Days of Christmas

Introduction

Christmas carols bring warmth and togetherness to the holiday season. And what celebration would be complete without *The Twelve Days of Christmas*, one of the best-loved songs of them all?

The Twelve Days of Christmas originated as a folk song in England and was first published around 1780. Both England and America have made the song their own by creating many variations of the lyrics and the music.

Here, wrapped in delightful full-color illustrations, we present to you the classic version of the classic carol. Whether you share it at home in front of a blazing fire, or while singing and stamping in the snow, this joyous tune is sure to add cheer and spirit to your holiday.

On the first day
of Christmas
my true love
gave to me
a partridge in
a pear tree.

On the second day
of Christmas
my true love
gave to me
two turtledoves,

On the third day
of Christmas
my true love
gave to me
three French hens,

two turtledoves,

On the fourth day
of Christmas
my true love
gave to me
four calling birds,

three French hens,
two turtledoves,

On the fifth day
of Christmas
my true love
gave to me
five golden rings,

four calling birds,
three French hens,
two turtledoves,

On the sixth day
of Christmas
my true love
gave to me
six geese a-laying,

five golden rings,
four calling birds,
three French hens,
two turtledoves,

On the seventh day
of Christmas
my true love gave to me
seven swans a-swimming,

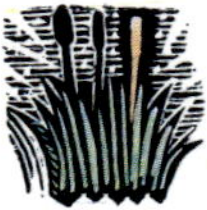

six geese a-laying,
five golden rings,
four calling birds,
three French hens,
two turtledoves,

On the eighth day
of Christmas
my true love gave to me
eight maids a-milking,

seven swans a-swimming,
six geese a-laying,
five golden rings,
four calling birds,
three French hens,

two turtledoves,

On the ninth day
   of Christmas
my true love gave to me
nine ladies dancing,

eight maids a-milking,
seven swans a-swimming,
six geese a-laying,
five golden rings,
four calling birds,

three French hens,

two turtledoves,

On the tenth day
of Christmas
my true love gave to me
ten lords a-leaping,

nine ladies dancing,
eight maids a-milking,
seven swans a-swimming,
six geese a-laying,
five golden rings,

four calling birds,
three French hens,
two turtledoves,

On the eleventh day
   of Christmas
my true love gave to me
eleven pipers piping,

ten lords a-leaping,
nine ladies dancing,
eight maids a-milking,
seven swans a-swimming,
six geese a-laying,

five golden rings,
four calling birds,
three French hens,
two turtledoves,

On the twelfth day
of Christmas
my true love
gave to me
twelve drummers
drumming,

eleven pipers piping,
ten lords a-leaping,
nine ladies dancing,
eight maids a-milking,
seven swans a-swimming,

six geese a-laying,
five golden rings,
four calling birds,
three French hens,
two turtledoves,

INTRODUCTION

THE HISTORY OF this tale is as rich as the story itself. Nearly two centuries ago, in 1816, the German writer E.T.A. Hoffman published a story called *The Nutcracker and the Mouse King*, telling how a little girl's love brought to life her cherished Nutcracker, an enchanted Christmas gift from her mysterious godfather.

In 1847, the French writer Alexandre Dumas published a retelling of Hoffman's story. From this adaptation, the Russian composers Peter Ilich Tchaikovsky and Lev Ivanov created their ballet, *The Nutcracker*, which was first performed in St. Petersburg in 1892.

Why has *The Nutcracker* remained so popular throughout the

world? As the story itself explains, "If you love something very much, it is always alive." Pure love of this extraordinary tale has kept the words alive for nearly two hundred years, so they can dance again for you across these colorful pages.

It had been snowing all day, and the gray city of Frankfurt was transformed. From her bedroom window Maria watched the white flakes falling, across tiled roofs and chimneys and steep gables, whirling against dark-leaded windows and laying a thick-piled carpet down every street and alley. The wind was rising, frequently blowing the snow in layers so dense as to hide the houses opposite. Then the layers would open up and you could see every lintel and cornice and ridge growing bigger and bigger with the snow.

Over a balcony of one house a carved stone head jutted out— the head of some soldier or hero, put there hundreds of years ago— but now, against the white drift lodged all around it, looking positively black like the face of a fierce Arab warrior staring out from under his white hood. In the gathering dusk Maria

was sure that the face was gazing right at her. How stern and frightening it looked!

Presently some lamps were lighted in a gallery of

windows next door, and in the bright beams the driven snow surged up like a crowd of elfin dancers in ballet dress. Waltzing and following fast on each other, they moved on in a mighty leap straight across the space toward Maria's window. She heard the tinkle of tiny diamonds upon the panes, she saw the fairylike figures, just for a moment, before a great blast of wind shook the old house and threw a blanket of snow against the glass.

Luckily, Maria thought, the fir tree had been brought to the door that morning—for it was Christmas eve—the party gifts had all been wrapped and the good things to eat prepared or delivered. But how will the guests ever get here through such a storm? The children, her cousins and friends, yes—but how about the grownups? There was to be a dance in the big room at the back of the house, and Maria could not bear to miss any of the ladies in their evening dresses.

And what of old Papa Drosselmeyer? He was godfather to both Maria and her brother Fritz. Christmas would not be Christmas without Godfather Drosselmeyer! Such a strange old man, so wise and so clever. So severe at times, in his black formal clothes, his old-fashioned manners and grave voice.

For years he had worn a dark patch over one eye—but the other eye was as staring and sharp as an owl's. And yet he was really lovable. No one else could tell such exciting stories, or bring such a feeling of wonder to every part of the festivities. And his presents were fantastic beyond belief—and each one made by himself. It was almost as if he were a magician!

Last year he had brought them a toy castle on a hill above a moat, and when you turned a crank a troop of knights rode up to the gate, the drawbridge was lowered, the great door opened, and out came a princess to receive her guests. There was a volley of cannons in salute, six of them, and the princess and the visiting captain of the knights went into the castle together. And before that, one year, there had been a magic theatre with two scenes from the Sleeping Beauty acted out by diminutive figures, and including a real little fountain that rose high in the air when the whole court awoke from its long sleep. And other inventions so precious that Father had had a special cupboard built to hold and keep them safe behind glass doors that locked. That cupboard, too, stood in the big room downstairs where the Christmas party always took place.

Maria unlatched the window and pushed it open against the snow piled on the sill. The icy white powder rushed up into her face and

into the room. But as she leaned out a little she could see some people with lanterns coming down the street. There were four grown people and several children. All bundled tight in heavy coats and bent into the storm. They looked funny because their feet were almost buried in the soft snow. And beyond them was another group. Surely that was her Aunt Lisa in the scarlet greatcoat! All of them were coming toward Maria Stahlbaum's house. The guests were beginning to arrive. Soon she and Fritz would be summoned, and the wonderful Christmas party would begin.

If only she could see Papa Drosselmeyer! He generally came in a carriage, but no carriage could get through this snow. Now there was another person coming, an old man—but no, that was Lawyer Handelman. He was stouter than Papa Drosselmeyer.

Suddenly Maria felt herself lifted from behind by two strong arms. She had to push hard with both hands against the icy sill to keep from toppling out. She struggled and kicked backward and came down in the room with a thud. She had scooped up a fistful of snow and held it menacingly toward her brother Fritz. He was always playing tricks like that. But he let her go, to dodge the snowball, which broke on the carpet behind him.

"Ria," he said, "Mr. and Mrs. Kretchma have come, with huge packages; Mr. and Mrs. Krone, with all their children, and the whole Zimmerman family. The children are in the front parlor, the others are finishing trimming the tree. Come on down the back stairs! You can see it all through the keyhole of the side door. The tree is the best we've ever had . . . and I think I have a real cannon . . .

and you have a doll with a big moustache!"

"You're making it up! No doll has a moustache."

"This one does, and a blue hat with a plume. It's a man doll, I guess, and I think he has a long sword . . . he must be a General."

"You're crazy! Who ever heard of a General doll?"

"I saw it," Fritz said. "And at any rate there is a table simply loaded with food—especially jellied meat and ham, chocolate cake, ginger cookies, and honey cakes. There are some of those buns with coffee icing. There are heaps of candy, peppermint stripes and all-colored bonbons. Come on!"

"Has Godfather come?"

"Godfather never comes

at the beginning. Don't you remember?"

"But will he come through this storm? He's so old and wrinkled . . . and then he has only one good eye."

"He'll come all right . . . with some mad present that has to be kept locked up. The snow won't keep him away. You know, I think he can fly like an owl and see in the dark. How he scares me sometimes! I'll bet he could fly right through that window ... Look out, here he comes!"

"Whoo—whoo," the blizzard shrieked against the windowpane. A chunk of solid snow dropped from the roof like a white owl upon the ledge outside. Fritz ran and locked the window tight, then grabbed his sister's hand, and both rushed laughing out of the room.

Maria was not really frightened by Fritz's pretending. She was a bit frightened by a mouse who

scurried out of sight as she and Fritz rushed down the hall. Dr. Stahlbaum's house was old and huge, there were a number of mice in the walls, and he was too kindhearted to trap them. Fritz did not mind them at all, but ever since Maria had seen one running off with a little rug from her doll house she did not like them. They were big blackish mice, too, and having such kind people to live with had made them very bold. They stayed up on the top floor particularly, because here were only Fritz's and Maria's rooms, some seldom occupied guest rooms, and some storage rooms at the rear. Sometimes at night, most often when the moon was shining, Maria would be wakened by the faint but persistent *cranch, cranch* of a mouse gnawing a hole behind her bureau or back of the wall.

There was a broad stairway going down to the family rooms on the floor below, and beyond that to the library, the sitting room and parlor. On the ground floor was Dr. Stahlbaum's office and

reception room, and also a little formal parlor where guests left their wraps. But a big house takes many people and much work to keep it tidy and spotlessly clean, so all of the rear part of the house was given over to kitchens and pantries, to a big dining room on the second floor, and servants' rooms above. And on the ground floor, running out like a wing into the garden, was the largest room in the house. It was a kind of drawing-room and play-room combined. You could reach it through the main hall on the ground floor, and you could also reach it by the back stairs, which was the way Fritz and Maria took now. Down six flights of crooked stairs they went, as quietly as possible, to the back hall, and then tiptoed along it to the side door of the big room.

When this house was built, long ago, doors often had keyholes as big as your middle finger, and since this door was a double one, the keyhole was extra large. Through it you could see almost all of the far

side of the room, the high wall with its paper pattern of somber garlands, the three very tall windows curtained in faded yellow and gold, the cupboard in the right corner where many of the children's toys were kept and—in locked doors above—Godfather Drosselmeyer's mechanical wonders. On the far left side you could almost see the owl-clock, standing six feet from the floor, all of carved wood. It struck the hours very solemnly, and was surmounted by a carved and painted owl, who opened his eyes and flapped his wings whenever the clock struck twelve.

But tonight not much of all this could be seen. For, as Maria looked, everything was at first blurred by people moving back and forth in the rooms. Her mother was there and some men and women all dressed for a party but as busy as squirrels, each one adding some bit to the

preparations. The carpet had been rolled back so people could dance; along the right side was a long table spread with a shining cloth and then platters and raised dishes of all kinds of refreshments.

Behind and above the people, in front of one window and nearly as tall, rose the Christmas tree. Its dark and beautiful branches curved out into the room, tier above tier, adorned with marvelous little toys of spangles and filigree, with glowing fruits of crimson and gold and violet, with fairy-tale angels and birds, with flowers of spun-glass, and with amusing cotton kittens and gnomes and animals of all kinds—so many that you could not possibly count them. And, in much the way that swags of snow might lie on a fir tree in the forest, gently weighing down the ends of its branches, a frosting of silver tinsel dipped from bough to bough in even curves, growing smaller as the tree narrowed upward, and holding it all—dark recesses and glitter of jewels—in a beautiful pattern. Near the top was a figure of Father Christmas, and at the very top a star.

"Now do you see the funny doll?" Fritz whispered, pushing against his sister.

"Wait a minute," she replied. "Isn't the tree wonderful! I can't look at anything else."

"Look down under it. There are lots of toys."

"There are too many people going back and forth. They must be nearly ready." Maria turned away.

"Fritz," she said, rather sternly, "we must go now and greet Clara and Karl and the others. They are probably all here by now. I hear them in the front hall."

Clara and Karl were only two of several cousins who had come to have Christmas Eve here. But they also knew about the side door and now came running in upon Fritz and Maria.

"Merry Christmas!" they called. "Oh, you're peeking! You're cheating! Let me look. Let me look."

And, pushing and shoving, as

overhasty people do, they all tried to look through the keyhole, no one having time enough to catch more than a blurred image before another child was close upon him trying to see, and finally all of them falling on top of one another in a mad scramble of giggles and acrobatics. They would have rolled in a heap, right into the room, had the door been suddenly opened.

But then the clock struck seven. They heard Mrs. Stahlbaum

calling: "Children, Father Christmas has come!" They just managed to disentangle themselves, to stand up and smooth out their party clothes, when the doors were thrown open wide. Maria's mother stood inside with her arms extended.

"Merry Christmas, my darlings," she said.

The tree had been lighted. Its glow and its fragrance filled the room. The star shone; every ornament twinkled.

"Merry Christmas," the children said softly.

Fritz and Maria stepped back to let the others go first into the room. The older people came forward to meet them, and all bowed formally to one another, for that was the custom in those times. One by one they greeted Dr. and Mrs. Stahlbaum. And though there were presents for all of them, it was the custom, too, for the children to have a little dance first, and then for the grownups to have a waltz, or perhaps a very gay dance called a galop, and then for young and old to dance together. Between dances they had glasses of punch, and Maria helped her mother pass the little cups around. Then they all sang a carol to the Christ Child, and it was time to have supper.

Nearly everyone was related or else quite old friends, so Maria knew everyone here. She did not see Papa Drosselmeyer. She kept looking, too, for the absurd doll that Fritz had described—but there was nothing like that among her presents. And now she was far too busy passing the cold meat and sandwiches and little cakes to think about her gift. But quite suddenly, as she offered some cake to old Mrs. Gumpel, who was sitting close to the tree, Maria saw on a little table beside the old lady the most remarkable thing.

Fritz had been telling the truth. Standing stiffly, as if at attention

—and quite gallantly, one felt—was a grotesque little soldier, an officer, in high polished boots, red trousers with a blue stripe, a white vest crossed by two bands of crimson, a deep blue General's coat, and an impressive hat with a plume. He must be made out of iron or some kind of metal, Maria thought, for he looked so sturdy and strong. He had a high-arched nose, a very full and almost pretty mouth, a jutting little chin, and very round and brave-looking eyes. He was no beauty, and—as Fritz had declared—a rather extra-large moustache grew from his upper lip but hardly adorned him. For all that, he held a long sword at his left side, and his eyes somehow had such a trusting and noble expression—brave and gentle at the same time—that Maria lost her heart to him at once.

Why, he is like a little prince! she thought. The soldier looked up at her steadily. His painted eyelashes gave him a very alert and appealing expression, somewhat like a big dog begging for a piece of your cake. How could anyone resist him? He made you feel protective and brave yourself.

" . . . Thank you, child," she heard Mrs. Gumpel saying. "The

almond torte is delicious...." The owl-clock struck again, and as it did so the door to the big hall opened slowly, and there stood Godfather Drosselmeyer. He was dressed all in black, with a gold chain around his neck. His white cravat and his hair like spun silver made the black suit look very sombre. He always wore a black patch over his left eye, but his other eye was so bright and piercing that it well served him for two. His usually white face was flushed with a rosy glow from the snowy night.

There he stood, bowing to the roomful of guests. And when he came forward he was followed by two menservants, each carrying a Christmas package nearly as big as a big boy. No one had ever seen such big packages before. When the greetings were over, the two servants untied and opened the packages. Out of one box they took a huge cabbage; out of the other a very pink cake, each about four feet high. Everyone crowded round in astonishment and curiosity.

The servants then lifted the cabbage and the cake, and underneath each was a doll nearly life-sized and all but real. They were dressed as a shepherd and shepherdess. They seemed to come alive; they rose and bowed to the audience and then to each other, and executed a most graceful and charming dance, ending by bowing low and sitting again in position ready for the green

cabbage and pink cake to cover them.

Of course everyone had to have them wound up and do their dance again, as they were just about the prettiest dolls in the world. When they had finished the second time and vanished under their covers, Godfather Drosselmeyer came over to Maria and Fritz. He bent to kiss each of them, and said:

"My dear godchildren, these creatures were made for you. They come to wish you a Happy Christmas, to give you old Drosselmeyer's love. He expects you to be very careful with them, as they are quite unique in this world and more delicately fashioned than any human being."

"Thank you, Godfather," they said together, "and Merry Christmas to you." But their thanks were nearly drowned out by the clamor of the other children begging for another performance of the dolls.

"No, no, my dears," the old man said. "Perhaps later on. There are other presents to be distributed."

"Can't we have the dancing dolls just once more, Godfather?" Maria asked.

"We must let Papa Drosselmeyer have his supper now, darling," Mother said. "Tomorrow you can have the dolls as long as you please."

So the cabbage and the cake were put away in a safe part of the cupboard. Drosselmeyer took Maria's hand affectionately.

"You know," he said, "I sent you and Fritz another little gift. Have you seen it? No? Well, look here!" And he went across toward the tree, past old Mrs. Gumpel, who was still munching sweet cakes, and picked up the brave iron soldier.

"Oh, I love him, Godfather," Maria cried. "Did you really make him for us?"

"For you and Fritz, yes. He is a nutcracker. Look! His jaws are so strong that he can crack the hardest nut without hurting his teeth at all."

Papa Drosselmeyer held the soldier with one hand and with his other hand raised the soldier's long sword backward. As he did so the pretty mouth opened wide revealing two rows of very white teeth. Then

Drosselmeyer placed a walnut in the nutcracker's mouth, pressed down the sword, and the jaw closed, cracking the shell into four even pieces so that the nutmeats were displayed quite ready to eat. He handed the cracked nut to Maria. Then he tried a hazelnut, an almond and a Brazil nut, each time giving the opened nut to one little girl or another. The boys, too, had crowded round to see this curious fellow. But Fritz was not much impressed.

"Didn't I tell you, Maria?" he said. "Now you have a doll with a big moustache!"

"He's not a doll. He's a magic nutcracker."

"What's so magic about him?" Fritz asked. He had never seen a nutcracker shaped like a soldier but he had seen silver ones, and a wooden one with a steel spring.

"Let me have him," he demanded. "I'll bet he can't crack every nut."

"No, you'll hurt him. Godfather, don't give him to Fritz."

"But I brought him for both of you, my dear. There, Fritz . . . and be careful. He'll crack your nuts for years, but you must not abuse him."

Thereupon Drosselmeyer turned away to speak with some older friends. Fritz held the little soldier high in the air and started putting nuts in his mouth and crushing them, one right after another.

Crack, crack, crack, crack went the little jaws, and nut after nut fell out perfectly bitten into four pieces. Then Fritz became annoyed and took an exceptionally large and heavy hickory nut, the toughest he could find in the dish, and pushed it far back into the soldier's mouth. *Crack, crack, crack,* . . . Fritz banged the sword up and down. The nut fell out, its shell severed in four even pieces, but there was a loose, clanking sound, and the little mouth fell open again, though no one had lifted the sword. Nutcracker was badly hurt.

"Fritz, you did it on purpose! You hurt him on purpose! How unhappy he looks now!"

Maria was dreadfully upset. Fritz laughed, to cover his shame, and turned away. But Maria took up Nutcracker in her arms and tried again and again to get his lower jaw into position. For Nutcracker seemed more real to her than did any of her dolls, and she felt certain he was in pain. What would she do now?

Papa Drosselmeyer had been watching her from across the room. He came over and shook his head sadly. Gently he took up Nutcracker and tried to set the broken jaw, but to no avail.

"He is badly hurt, Maria," he said. "But he is only wounded, and perhaps we can heal the wound in time. Let us bandage it well and give him some rest."

Taking a large linen handkerchief from his coat pocket, Drosselmeyer bound it firmly around the jaw, holding it in position as he did so.

"With love and good care he may recover. I rather think he will, dear. Now put him down and enjoy the rest of the party."

Maria went to the toy cupboard, where one of her doll's beds stood on the lowest shelf. She turned back the pink coverlet and white sheet, and smoothed out the pillow. It was just the right size for Nutcracker. Very gently she made him comfortable in the bed, lying on his side; and she was not at all surprised when his eyes closed as she laid him

down. He had no fever, she could tell. He could sleep now. In the morning she would come to look after him and bring him some nourishment.

Meanwhile the party had become very merry. People were laughing and talking gaily. Only the figure of Papa Drosselmeyer made a serious note as he moved slowly among the brightly dressed ladies and men.

Coming back from the cupboard, Maria saw that the presents had just been given. For each girl a handsomely dressed doll, with a doll's blanket and pillow. For each boy a little rifle, and either a drum or a fife. Soon the girls were rocking their new babies in their arms, and the boys, led by Fritz, formed into a platoon of well-drilled troops and went parading back and forth across the room, shrill fifes piercing the air and drum-rolls thundering out over all conversation. On they came, in battle array, and suddenly making a left-march plunged head-on into the group of girls with their dolls. The girls screamed. Maria started scolding Fritz, and in two minutes there was more noise in the room than in the wild storm outside.

At length Fritz's father could tolerate it no

longer. "Stop it, stop it," he cried. "This is a party for everyone, not just for boys and girls. Come all of you now and take partners. We need another dance."

Aunt Lisa sat at the square piano, and soon they were all off in a lively polka. It was great fun, and had to be followed by an easier and less strenuous waltz. Then the ices and rich mocha cake were served. Or you could have fruitcake and coffee or tea, or hot chocolate for most of the children. Some of the grown people had wine, and they all offered toasts to each other and to Christmas itself. They stood in front of the tree and sang the carol of Christmas Night.

It was time to be going. Old Mrs. Gumpel was already nodding, and several boys were struggling manfully to keep from yawning. The warm room, the rich food, the dancing had made everyone a bit tired. So into their winter wraps and out into the snowy night they all went, with such fond farewells that you would have thought there is no time so wonderful as Christmas time — and you would have been right.

The last to come and the last to leave: that was Papa Drosselmeyer. Long after the children were in their beds Mother and Father stood in the front hall saying good-night to lingering guests. It was getting chilly from the constant opening of the outer door. And only when everyone else had gone did Drosselmeyer appear—at the far end of the hall, not from the cloak room, although he was covered from shoulders to shoes in an immense fur coat with cloth buttons and yards of black braid. There was a crafty glint in his eye.

"Well, you have made an old man feel young again," he said to his hosts. "What a splendid and joyous evening! Truly, a spell was put upon this house tonight."

He shook hands with them. He

put on his tall fur hat and stood on the top step. The snowstorm swirled down around him and he seemed to vanish in it like a wizard.

Days later a maid, who had come back into the empty party room that night to tidy up a bit, when the last guests were departing, said she had been badly frightened by finding a little old man there, in the corner, bending over a doll's bed. He had a slender shining object in one hand, like a medicine dropper or a small screwdriver. When she called out he just raised one finger to his lips and made the sign of silence. In the dim room the maid was too startled to know if it was one of the guests— she thought it could not possibly be.

Cranch, cranch . . . cranch . . . there was that sound in the walls again.

Maria sat up in bed, holding the quilt around her. How cold it was, and how silent . . . except for that

amiliar noise of the mischievous mice. The snow had stopped falling and the moon must have come out. She could see it glinting on the tiny tinsel wrapper of a candy on her bed table. She had brought it up for a good-night snack and had been too sleepy to eat it. She felt wide awake now, though she could not have slept very long, for it was deep night.

Cranch, cranch—she had never heard the sound so loud. Were they bigger mice? Or were there more of them?

She leaned from her bed to look at the sky. The moon hung up there, like a silver Christmas-tree ball. But how cold it appeared! And how cold the room was! Well, she must pull up her extra quilt and go to sleep again.

And then she thought of the Christmas tree and of Nutcracker lying in his little bed with its thin cover. She wished she had brought him up here. Surely she should have given him more covers, for the party room would be bitterly cold by now.

Maria slid out of bed, into her slippers and wrapper. She pulled it tight around her. She lighted her bedside candle-lamp. The sound in the walls stopped abruptly. She opened the door quietly and went down the long hall. The lamp threw leaping shadows to left and to right and behind her but kept opening up the way ahead.

Since the wind had fallen, there

was not a sound outside or inside the house. Maria's velvet slippers muffled her steps. She could only hear, as if from far away, the faint whisper of her nightclothes as she moved. The stairs were carpeted and firm. She went down them in silence.

Even going into the big room made no sound, for the door was ajar and she could pass through. Behind the door most of the room lay in shadow; her candle beam lighted only a narrow strip of the floor. As she came in it followed across to the wainscot, up the tall owl-clock. It picked out the dial and then both golden hands pointing together to the owl's head on top.

The owl stirred and opened its eyes, and at that very instant the clock spoke—a loud, deep and hollow O-o-o-o that reverberated from wall to wall. The owl raised itself up and began beating its wings, or was it Godfather Drosselmeyer there behind the clock, looking quite angry, his long coattails flapping? The clock struck again, and again, as Maria went on to the toy cupboard. In front of it was the doll's bed. And there was Nutcracker sound asleep. To her great joy, his mouth was peacefully closed and the bandage had slipped off. He would get well!

She started to take him up in her arms ... and there came that sound, very faintly, *cranch, cranch* ... *cranchety-cranch*.

Maria stood up.

The sound came again, closer

and louder, *cranch, cranch!* And it was followed by the rattle of tiny running feet.

A mouse's face appeared under the Christmas tree, and vanished. Then another, much nearer. Oh what a big and ugly mouse! He seemed to be getting larger and coming straight for Maria.

At this moment her candle went out. A score of wicked little mouse eyes danced around the room. Terrified, Maria threw herself on the sofa and buried her face in the pillows.

When she looked out again there was a strange dim light all over the room. She could not tell where it came from. Many figures were moving back and forth in a kind of planned activity, as if following orders. They were mice— but far larger than any mice ever seen before. They were quite fat and nearly black, with long stringy tails. They had sharp knives like

swords, and they were assembling on the side of the room opposite the toy cupboard.

Trying to discover where the light came from, Maria now noticed the strangest thing. Not only the mice, but the sofa, the table and chairs, the cupboard were getting larger and larger. The Christmas tree boughs reached out into the room and upwards, the needles growing much longer, and all the ornaments blowing out like balloons but keeping their various forms. The tinsel garlands were thick ropes of silver and gold. The doll's bed —and Nutcracker in it—were becoming nearly life-size. The room itself was expanding.

Or was Maria growing smaller and smaller? She felt the sofa rising up beneath her. The seat was already about six feet from the floor. She had better get off right away. She slid down the curving leg, and touched the floor just a few feet from her doll's bed, which was now roomy enough for Maria herself. Nutcracker was gone!

Now the room was in great commotion. The mice, as large as big dogs, were looking very unfriendly. Their bulky forms were crowding together across the room, lining up in regular rows. One of them gave a high shriek, flourished his knife, and the whole band came charging toward the cupboard. Their wiry black feet made that scratchy sound Maria knew so well, only much louder.

In another second the mice would have been upon her. But a bugle sounded, the cupboard doors opened, and a troop of wooden soldiers as large as the mice rushed out to engage them. Cannons were wheeled into position, and ball after ball—red, pink, white, and blue—was sent in showers against the mice. But how strangely soft they were, more like big gumdrops. They seemed only to bounce off the fat mice's fur.

The bugle sounded again.

The soldiers collected in three rows. The front row of troops had painted swords, the second had little rifles, the third had rifles with bayonets. And a noble figure suddenly appeared at the head of the troops, in red trousers, blue coat, and plumed head dress. It was Nutcracker.

He had drawn his sword He turned halfway round

to the first line of troops, gave a command, and led them straight into the front ranks of the mouse army. What fierce hand-to-hand combat followed! The soldiers stood there bravely, but their tin swords were no match for the knives and sharp teeth of the mice, and many soldiers were severely scratched and bitten.

Cranch, cranch, sounded the mouse battle-cry.

Nutcracker signaled again, and

the second line of soldiers ran into the fight. Pausing a few feet from their huddled foes, they all fell to their knees and took aim. The savage mouse horde came on then, eyes and teeth flashing. At close range the riflemen fired. Unfortunately their courage was not matched by arms of sufficient power, and the shot only tickled and prickled the tough skins of the mice. One or two squealed in pain, the rest were only made the more angry, whereas several soldiers lost an arm or a leg to the infuriated foe.

Nutcracker now summoned his last defenses. The third rank came on at a run, guns lowered and sharp steel bayonets thrust forward. The mouse brigands did not move and were about to be pierced through and through when they dropped on all fours and scampered cunningly between the soldiers' legs, upsetting many of them, grappling them firmly by both legs, and carrying them off as prisoners.

It seemed certain now that the toy cupboard, with all its treasures, would fall victim to the mouse army. And, to make matters worse, at this moment appeared a horrible creature, largest of all the mice, of a disgusting dirty-gray color, his terrible eyes flashing from left to right, his whiskers vibrating with rage. He wore a bizarre headdress of seven mouse-heads, each with its golden crown. He was the Mouse King. He put himself at the front of his cut-throat band, puffed himself up with pride, and prepared to lead them all up to the cupboard.

Nutcracker, rather badly battered, was in the center of the room, directly in the Mouse King's path. He stood, as usual, both feet planted together, and drew out his long, strong sword.

The Mouse King had a club—black and rusty and stained, and dreadful to look at. And he had his very large and protruding sharp teeth.

I do not suppose there has ever been such a curious and furious encounter. It was the Mouse King's method to feign a terrific blow with his club and then to dart under his raised weapon and give his foe a savage bite. But, trying this on Nutcracker, who was made of iron, the Mouse King hurt his teeth so severely that he became enraged and then took up his black club in both hands and began beating Nutcracker mercilessly. Meanwhile the brave soldier set about warding off the club and quickly following that by a sharp thrust at his enemy's fat belly. But for all his fatness Mouse King was the quickest and wiliest of his tribe, and so expert at twisting and dodging and leaping and ducking this way and that, that Nutcracker could only touch him lightly here and there. All the time he had to keep fending off the blows of that terrible club. Down, down, the blows kept falling on Nutcracker's head and shoulders.

Then it occurred to Nutcracker that he might get at his enemy's legs, but so swift were they at jumping and tripping, so incessantly restless, that Nutcracker could not really see one foot or the other long enough to judge his aim properly.

Maria had been watching the

combat from her place at the sofa. She saw that Nutcracker could not last much longer. But she had no gun and no sword. What could she do?

Nutcracker staggered back one step. The terrible club kept pummeling him, till he felt he would suddenly crack in two.

Maria could stand it no longer. Her fear for

Nutcracker now made her both cunning and bold. She took off one velvet slipper. Even the heel was not very hard, not much of a weapon. But perhaps she could use it well. She ran up to the Mouse King, no longer afraid, and as he lifted his club high over his head, rushed in and threw the slipper right at his face.

Astonished and enraged, Mouse King deserted his opponent and raced after Maria. That was just what she had wanted, for immediately Nutcracker came up behind him and stuck his sword deep into the monstrous King.

Maria bounced into her doll's bed. She was not at all hurt.

Nutcracker stood perfectly still for a moment. He was overcome with weariness and relief. His deep-drawn breathing was the only sound in the room—or was it the thudding of his heart? He put away his sword. Suddenly he toppled right over, without bending, like a toy.

The horde of mice, who had thought their

monarch invincible, fell down in grief and terror at his death.
In another moment they gathered up his swollen body in their arms, and fled. You could hear the scampering of their wiry feet, even after the last one had disappeared. Where they went, or how they went, is a mystery. All we know is that their wicked little eyes

were never seen in that house again.

Maria saw that Nutcracker had fainted, and started toward him, when he stirred and opened his eyes. He raised himself on one arm. Then he stood up, restored.

Restored not only to his full strength but to his true self—he no longer was dressed like a soldier, he no longer had a moustache and high-arched nose. He was a very handsome youth dressed in long azure-blue hose, a jerkin and slippers of silver, and a little cloak lined with crimson. His hair was cut close, of a ruddy blond color almost matching his belt

and scabbard of gold. Only his eyes had not changed. They were as deep and round and confident as before.

"Is it you, Nutcracker?" Maria said, so astonished she could only stand and stare. "What does it all mean?"

He smiled at her very tenderly. Then he looked at his different clothes.

"It means," he said, "that the spell has been broken. I was a young boy who did not appreciate his good fortune. I had health and friends and work to do—but I was so foolish as to be discontented and to complain of this and of that all the time. An enchanter deprived me of the power of speech and turned me into a nutcracker, so that my mouth would no longer whine but would serve some kind of purpose. Until I should learn to be glad of living and being of use. Until someone should realize how much I had changed and believe that I had a new heart under my funny costume of painted iron.... It was you, Maria, who broke the enchantment—or rather, completed it, since now I do know that it is good and wonderful to be alive.... For, you see, it was a lucky enchantment.... But there you stand, with only one slipper on ... and where is your wrapper?"

Nutcracker crossed to the far corner of the room and found the velvet slipper that had saved his life, and then to the opposite side, where Maria's wrapper hung over the foot of the bed. He put the wrapper around her. She sat on the edge of the bed

and he put the slipper on her foot.

The room became illuminated from outside as the moon began to shine on the snow and was reflected through the window. It shone on Maria's slipper and on the golden sword at Nutcracker's side. It shone on all the ornaments of the Christmas tree.

"What is your real name?" Maria asked.

"My name is Prince Nikita, but now I like Nutcracker better."

"And what are you going to do?"

"I think I shall go on being a nutcracker," he said. "That is as good a job as any, at least for a while. And, as a matter of fact, I have become rather proud of my very strong jaws."

"But if you are a prince you must live far away, Nutcracker. Will you go there?"

"No, I want to stay here with you, Maria. Where I live is quite

far away, if you *think* it is far away.
But it is only a few steps really.

Come, I will show you."

One of the tall French windows blew open. The moon had disappeared and there was a new flurry of snow. Nutcracker lifted his beautiful sword and walked out into the night.

Maria was spellbound for a moment. And then as she was about to rise and follow him, her little bed began to move like a sleigh toward the window. She pulled up her knees; she tucked the wrapper and the coverlet close around her. But she was quite warm. Without a sound her bed glided on, under the yellow curtains, out of doors.

Have you ever been in a forest

in deep winter? With the snow frozen so hard you can walk on its glassy surface, with green fir trees and pine trees wearing edgings of snow like white fur, and slender birches like fountains of frost? Little tracks of rabbits and birds crisscross on the white floor, and minute crystals of ice go on and off like winter fireflies. The trees interlace in carved arches overhead and all around make a mysterious labyrinth. It is so still you can hear the least movement of twig or shifting of snow.

Through such a forest Maria found herself moving in her sleigh-bed. Nutcracker strode on ahead, his red cloak a beckoning torch. It was no longer night, and it was snowing again—large flakes that circled around the bed and came rushing toward it in a great throng at every new turn in the path. Then Maria saw what she had only glimpsed from the window hours

ago—the Snow Fairies soaring through the air and dancing down the aisles of the forest. She thought them extraordinarily lovely: their transparent complexions, their costumes of hoarfrost and silver, their diadems of snowflakes more brilliant than diamonds. In ever-increasing numbers they surrounded the sleigh-bed, whirling and leaping so close together that it was quite dizzying. They became a blur of movement, indistinguishable from the falling snow.

And then, at the height of their

wild dance, the forest and all its spirits seemed to melt into air. The snow was gone. The path had become a little canal of water bordered with green plants and flowers. The bed was a boat upon it. Far down the canal, Maria could see a flight of stairs at one side, with Nutcracker waiting on the lowest step. As the little boat-bed drew up, he stepped aboard beside Maria, and they sailed on.

Now in the distance a castle

seemed to rise out of the water. It gleamed like a giant-size party cake and was reflected in the still water. Its walls were of sugar icing; over the windows were candy flowers; and peppermint stripes spiraled up the tall towers. At intervals stood statues, carved out of marzipan.

An archway of golden taffy spanned the canal, and under it the boat glided into the castle. It stopped at a flight of broad steps, in a great hall that was made entirely of rock candy in soft pinks and yellows. Columns of clear rock candy surrounded the room; the floor was a sheet of candy like glass.

A stately lady dressed in gleaming white satin stood at the top of the stairs to receive them, and beyond were many men and women dressed as if for a ball.

Nutcracker seemed to know the lady quite well. He said that she was the Sugar Plum Fairy and that this was the Fortress of Sweets. He introduced Maria, and then he explained to everyone how Maria had saved his life and broken the magic spell. All the courtiers said she had been very brave.

The Sugar Plum Fairy now escorted the children to a table on a platform that overlooked the rock-candy hall. Places were set for supper; and presently people brought in the most delicious and unusual food. For, after their battle with the mice and their trip through the forest, Nutcracker and Maria were mighty hungry. Each new kind of refreshment was so prettily decorated and shaped that you could not tell just what it was. But it was better than ice cream, or cherry pie, or any birthday cake.

While they sat having this delectable feast, the court devoted itself to entertaining them. There was music and a series of clever dances, each representing something good to eat or to drink. Two women in ruffled skirts and two men in tight flaring trousers did the dance of Chocolate, which was really a Spanish dance, because much chocolate comes, or used to come, from Spain.

A stern-looking Arab did a slow and rather sleepy dance on a prayer rug. The music and his languid movements made you see the hot and lonely desert at night. Servants gave him tiny cups of coffee now and then, for the Arabians are great coffee drinkers.

To the weird sound of elfin bells

and reed pipes two Chinese girls brought in a big box of bamboo, like a tea chest. Out of it suddenly vaulted two Asian acrobats. Around and around the candy hall they turned cartwheels and flipflops. They pranced and jumped and made mighty leaps into space. One of them vaulted right over the table where Nutcracker and Maria were sitting. This dance was called the dance of Tea, because Chinese people especially love that drink.

In came a number of muscular young men dressed in red and white stripes, and carrying hoops. This was a dance of great agility and speed. The men seemed to fly through the air and to dive through their whirling hoops. It was the most brilliant dance of all.

But now came the most amusing one. How Fritz would have liked it! Maria thought. A very tall woman came jerkily in, wearing the most tremendous skirt, like a huge round candy box. Suddenly she lifted one part of her skirt, and out came the tiniest roly-polies, who tumbled and tripped about, each just like a dainty bonbon. You would think surely there was nothing but soft cream and almonds inside them. They were dressed in pink, and

lavender, pale green, pale yellow,
and coffee color, and there were
quantities of them! But
somehow they all
managed to crowd
back under the big
skirts again, and the
candy-box lady
sidled off.

The music
changed to an airy and soaring
waltz. And as it did so a troop
of dancers looking like flowers

floated softly down from balconies and windows between the clear-sugar columns. They seemed to have no weight at all, only the delicacy and purity of wild things. They danced as if borne up by a

breeze, and made you think of a mountain meadow. finally, like dandelion seeds, they were wafted up, one after the other, and out between the columns.

Now the Sugar Plum Fairy came forward, with a handsome man of the court, to show what they could do. And this was the best of all, dancing so wonderful that Nutcracker and Maria forgot their caramel sherbet and sat enraptured.

Only a dancer, I think, could describe the grandeur and charm of those figures, responding to each other and to the music in perfect unison, creating a pattern of motion that seemed to fill the vast room with varying advances and retreats, curves and reverse curves, vigor and grace, till you were hypnotized by its splendor. They danced together; they danced alone. And at the climax the Sugar Plum Fairy spun like a top at

furious speed all the length of the room and was caught and lifted up triumphantly by her partner.

When the applause had subsided the two dancers smiled and beckoned for Nutcracker and Maria to come down. All of the court gathered round, and the children thanked them, bowing low.

As Maria raised her head she knew that the court was not there. The light, too, was different. The crystalline floor was the white quilt of her bed at home.

She opened her eyes wide. The clear light of morning was streaming into her room. An icicle glittered outside the window pane, and beyond, the sky was intensely blue. Snow was blowing off the rooftops like smoke. There was a faint smell of toast and coffee from downstairs.

Then she saw, near the fireplace, her doll's bed. And Nutcracker lying in it, in his General's uniform.

His sword and his plumed hat were at the foot of the bed. Maria stared at him. He seemed to have just awakened, too, and he was looking right at her. She thought that he smiled.

The door to the hall opened, and mother came in with a tray.

"How late you have slept, Maria! And on Christmas morning! The storm is over, and the whole world is washed clean. You never saw such a beautiful Christmas Day."

She came over and kissed Maria.

"I've brought you breakfast in bed, for we are all through downstairs.... Do you feel well?"

"Yes, Mother, I do, and thank you for breakfast. What a party it was!... I was so excited I don't remember bringing Nutcracker upstairs."

"No, darling, I brought him up early this morning. And one of your slippers. The big room was in such a state...there were gumdrops all over the floor!"

"Tell me, Mother," Maria asked, "is Godfather Drosselmeyer a magician?"

"Of course not. He is just a clever and ingenious man who is very fond of you."

"But how did he bring Nutcracker alive?"

"If Nutcracker came alive, it was because you liked him so well. If you love something very much it is

always alive.... What a funny child you are today! Now get washed and have your breakfast. I'll light the fire."

The Night Before Christmas

Introduction

A red-suited Santa in a reindeer-drawn sleigh, a never-empty sack of toys, and stockings hung expectantly above the fireplace—so many of our Christmas traditions were spun together in 1822 by a New York clergyman named Clement Clarke Moore in *A Visit from St. Nicholas*.

Originally written for Moore's own children, the poem was published anonymously in a newspaper in Troy, New York. It quickly became fixed in the public imagination. The poem's opening line—"'Twas the night before Christmas"—became so famous that it replaced the original title.

One reason Moore's poem has endured is

that it's a joy to read aloud. Beginning in hushed suspense, the poem builds to a dramatic crescendo as rollicking verses usher in the mysterious midnight visitor. A reading of this poem on Christmas Eve has for many families become a holiday tradition in itself.

'Twas the night before Christmas, when all through the house

Not a creature

was stirring,

not even a mouse;

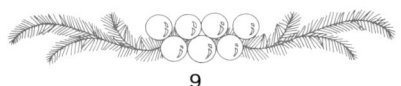

The stockings
were hung
by the chimney
with care,

In hopes that

St. Nicholas

soon would be there.

The children
were nestled
all snug
in their beds,

While visions

of sugarplums

danced in their heads;

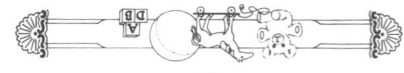

And Mama

in her kerchief

and I in my cap,

Had just
settled down
for a long
winter's nap~

When out
on the lawn
there rose
such a clatter,

I sprang
from my bed
to see what
was the matter.

Away to the window

I flew

like a flash,

Tore open
the shutters
and threw
up the sash.

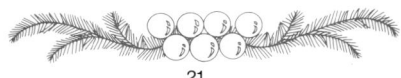

The moon

on the breast

of the new-fallen snow,

Gave a luster

of midday

to objects below;

When, what

to my wondering

eyes should appear,

But a
miniature sleigh
and eight
tiny reindeer,

With a little
old driver
so lively
and quick,

I knew
in a moment
it must be
St. Nick.

More rapid
than eagles
his coursers
they came,

And he whistled,
and shouted,
and called them
by name –

"Now, Dasher!
Now, Dancer!
Now, Prancer
and Vixen!

On, Comet!
      On, Cupid!
On, Donder
      and Blitzen!

To the top
>   of the porch,
to the top
>   of the wall!

Now, dash away!

Dash away!

Dash away all!"

As dry leaves

before the

wild hurricane fly,

When they meet

with an obstacle,

mount to the sky,

So up
to the housetop
the coursers
they flew,

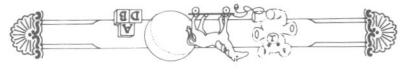

With sleigh

full of toys –

and St. Nicholas too;

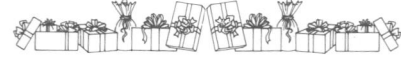

And then

in a twinkling,

I heard on the roof

The prancing

and pawing

of each little hoof.

As I drew in my head

and was

turning around,

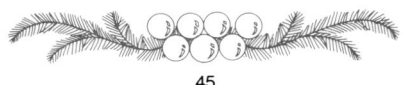

Down the chimney

St. Nicholas

came with a bound.

He was dressed
all in fur
from his head
to his foot,

And his clothes
were all tarnished
with ashes and soot.

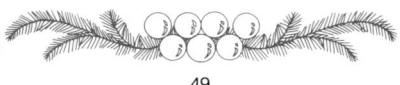

A bundle of toys

he had flung

on his back,

And he looked
like a peddler
just opening
his pack.

His eyes
how they twinkled!
His dimples
how merry!

His cheeks
were like roses,
his nose
like a cherry!

His droll little mouth
was drawn up
like a bow,

And the beard
on his chin
was as white
as the snow!

The stump of a pipe

he held tight

in his teeth,

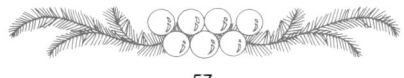

And the smoke
it encircled
his head
like a wreath.

He had
a broad face
and a little
round belly

That shook
when he laughed
like a bowl
full of jelly.

He was chubby

and plump –

a right jolly old elf,

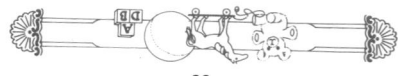

And I laughed

when I saw him,

in spite of myself.

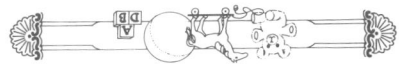

A wink of his eye

and a twist

of his head,

Soon gave me
to know
I had nothing
to dread.

He spoke
not a word,
but went straight
to his work,

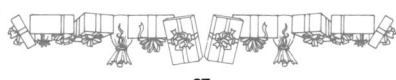

And filled
all the stockings
then turned
with a jerk,

And laying

his finger

aside of his nose,

And giving a nod,

up the chimney

he rose.

He sprang
to his sleigh,
to his team
gave a whistle,

And away
they all flew
like the down
of a thistle.

But I heard
him exclaim
as he drove
out of sight,

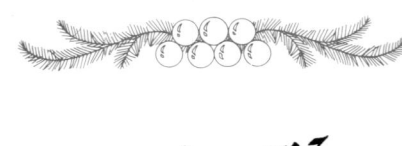

"Merry Christmas to all